HORSE ANATOMY

John Green

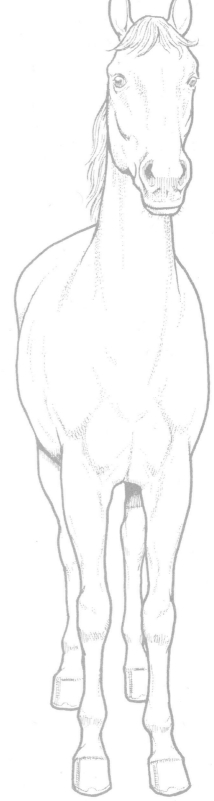

Dover Publications, Inc.
Mineola, New York

Copyright

Copyright © 2006 by Dover Publications, Inc.
All rights reserved.

Bibliographical Note

Horse Anatomy is a new work, first published by Dover Publications, Inc., in 2006.

International Standard Book Number

ISBN-13: 978-0-486-44813-8
ISBN-10: 0-486-44813-4

Manufactured in the United States by Courier Corporation
44813407
www.doverpublications.com

1. The Evolution of the Horse

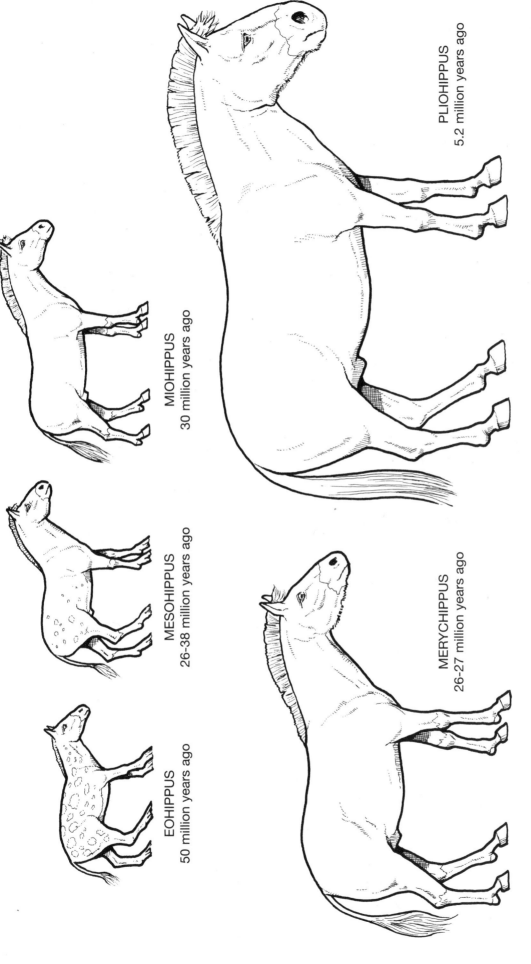

EOHIPPUS
50 million years ago

MESOHIPPUS
26-38 million years ago

MIOHIPPUS
30 million years ago

MERYCHIPPUS
26-27 million years ago

PLIOHIPPUS
5.2 million years ago

The horse as we know it today is the product of a long evolutionary chain stretching back millions of years. The chain begins with eohippus, or "dawn horse," a small animal which flourished over fifty million years ago. Eohippus was equipped with four toes on its forefeet and three toes on its hind feet, all terminating in thick horn. Behind the toes was a pad, which persists in the modern horse as a small, horny callosity on the point of the fetlock, called the "ergot." Scientists know what eohippus looked like because a nearly complete skeleton was discovered in Wyoming in 1931.

Over millions of years, the multiple toes on the horses' feet gradually evolved into a single toe as the size of the digits decreased until only the central one played any part in running. The first one-toed horses were grazers, like their three-toed ancestors. Over time, horses also increased in size, from the hare-sized eohippus, to the large animals we know today. As horses adapted to their environment, changes in the skull and limbs also took place. The first horses were domesticated around 3,000 B.C., probably in Asiatic Russia.

2. Points of the Horse

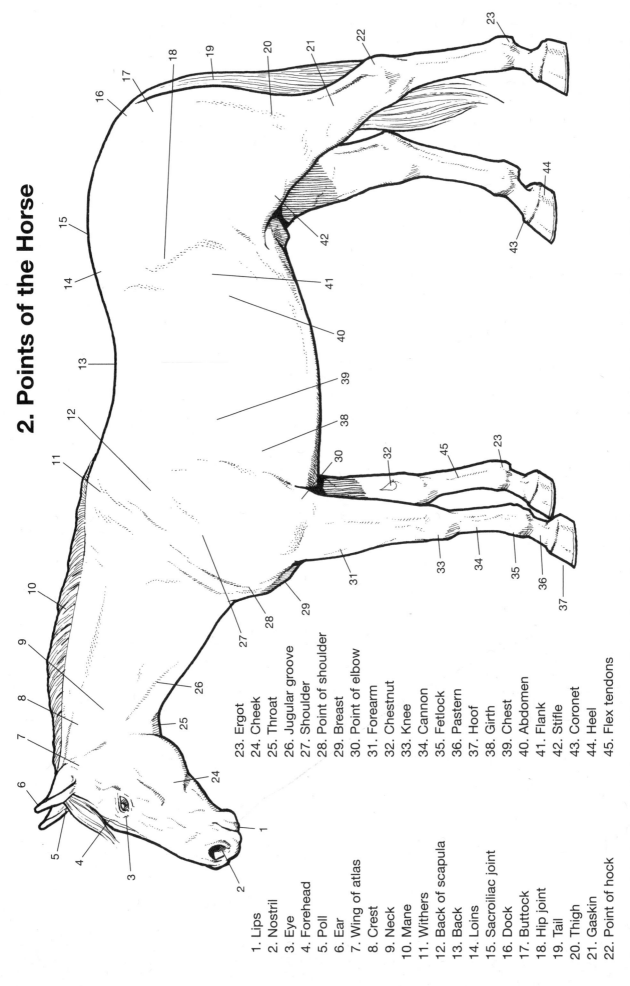

1. Lips
2. Nostril
3. Eye
4. Forehead
5. Poll
6. Ear
7. Wing of atlas
8. Crest
9. Neck
10. Mane
11. Withers
12. Back of scapula
13. Back
14. Loins
15. Sacroiliac joint
16. Dock
17. Buttock
18. Hip joint
19. Tail
20. Thigh
21. Gaskin
22. Point of hock

23. Ergot
24. Cheek
25. Throat
26. Jugular groove
27. Shoulder
28. Point of shoulder
29. Breast
30. Point of elbow
31. Forearm
32. Chestnut
33. Knee
34. Cannon
35. Fetlock
36. Pastern
37. Hoof
38. Girth
39. Chest
40. Abdomen
41. Flank
42. Stifle
43. Coronet
44. Heel
45. Flex tendons

The points of the horse are the external features that make up the horse's conformation, or shape. Knowledge of the points of the horse is vital for a real understanding of the animal. Experts acquire this knowledge by visual examination and physical touch. By feeling the point of the shoulder and other associated features, for instance, it is possible to establish what the angle of the shoulder is and whether it is correctly conformed. No one feature should be out of proportion with the others.

3. The Skin

The skin is the largest organ of the horse's body. It is made up of tissue known as the epithelium, which consists of two distinct layers. The uppermost is the epidermis, an avascular, keratin-rich layer of protective covering, divided into two sub-layers: the outer, called the stratum corneum, and the inner, called the stratum germinativum. The deeper skin layer is the dermis, or corium, the flexible, nourishing source of the epidermis. It is an intricately woven layer of collagen strands, elastic fibers, and fat, including hair follicles, sweat and sebaceous glands, and the udder in the female. Blood and lymph vessels, muscles, and nerves are embedded at various levels.

1. Pore
2. Hair
3. Epidermis
4. Nerve ending
5. Dermis
6. Hypodermis
7. Subcutaneous fat
8. Apocrine sweat gland
9. Blood vessel
10. Hair bulb
11. Hair follicle
12. Motor nerve
13. Arrector pili muscle

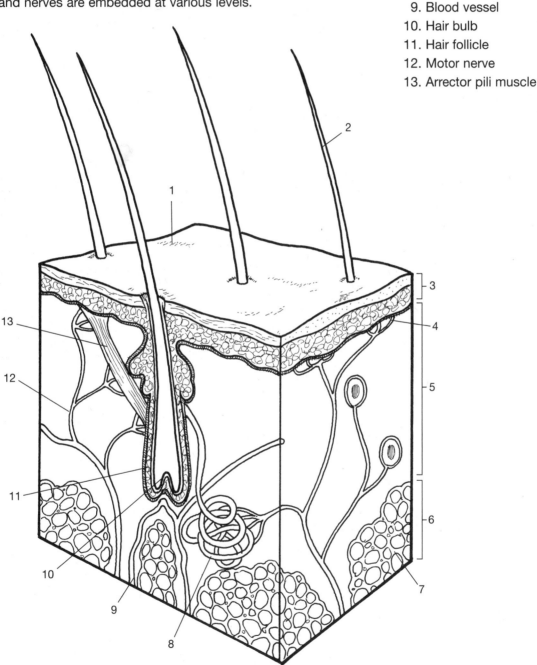

Among the many functions of the skin, two are especially important: it is a barrier to harmful microorganisms, and it offers protection from the elements. The hair over much of its surface grows in "streams" that help repel rain and sweat. In addition, the skin of the horse contains sebaceous glands, which produce an oily material that waterproofs the skin. Horses are quite susceptible to skin problems, however, especially in unhygienic conditions, and good stable and field management are essential.

4. The Muscles of the Horse

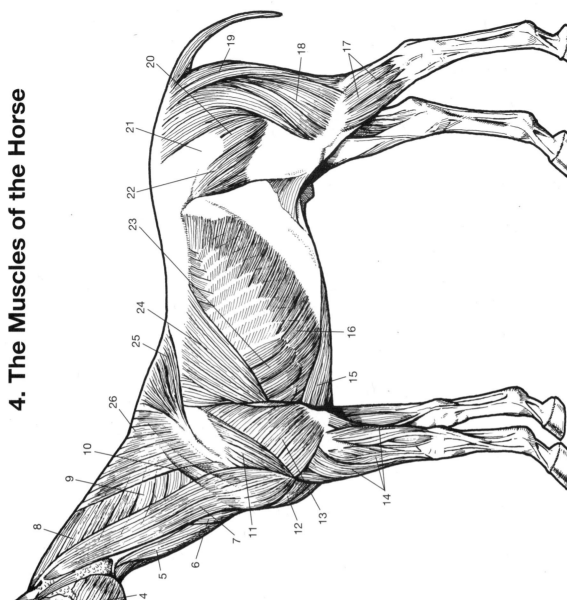

1. Superior labial levator muscle
2. Canine muscle
3. Nasolabial levator muscle
4. Masseter muscle
5. Sternomandibular muscle
6. Cervical cutaneous muscle
7. Brachiocephalic muscle
8. Splenius muscle
9. Cervical ventral serrated muscle
10. Subclavian muscle
11. Deltoid muscle
12. Descending pectoral muscle
13. Brachial triceps
14. Carpal and digital extensor muscles
15. Ascending pectoral muscle
16. External abdominal oblique muscle
17. Digital extensor muscles
18. Femoral biceps muscles
19. Semitendinous muscle
20. Superficial gluteal muscle
21. Gluteal fascia
22. Tensor muscle
23. Thoracic ventral serrated muscle
24. Latissimus dorsi muscle
25. Thoracic trapezius muscle
26. Cervical trapezius muscle

There are approximately 700 separate muscles in a horse's body. All movements, from a flick of the tail to the most difficult maneuver, are brought about by a complicated system of skeletal muscles. Motion is produced by the contraction and relaxation of alternating, opposing groups of muscles acting reciprocally on skeletal layers and eventually on the hooves as fulcrums on the ground.

Centuries of selective breeding have led to enhanced muscular development in some breeds and types. For example, the quarter horse, bred to sprint, has highly developed, muscular forelimbs and hindquarters, while the *steeplechasing* thoroughbred, bred to race over courses with hurdles and water jumps, has a less muscular physique than the *sprinting* thoroughbred.

5. The Deeper Muscles of the Horse

1. Longest capital and atlantal muscle
2. Complex muscle
3. Rhomboid muscle
4. Thoracic spinal muscle
5. Iliocostal muscle
6. Longest dorsal muscle
7. Caudal dorsal serrated muscle
8. Omohyoid muscle
9. Cervical ventral serrated muscle
10. Thoracic ventral serrated muscle
11. Subclavian muscle
12. Supraspinate muscle
13. Infraspinate muscle
14. Brachial biceps muscle
15. Long head of brachial triceps muscle
16. Lateral head of brachial triceps muscle
17. External intercostal muscles
18. Transverse abdominal muscles
19. Internal abdominal oblique muscles
20. External abdominal oblique muscle
21. Iliac muscle
22. Femoral quadriceps muscle
23. Middle gluteal muscle
24. Semimembranous muscle
25. Semitendinous muscle
26. Gastrocnemius muscle

6. The Horse in Motion

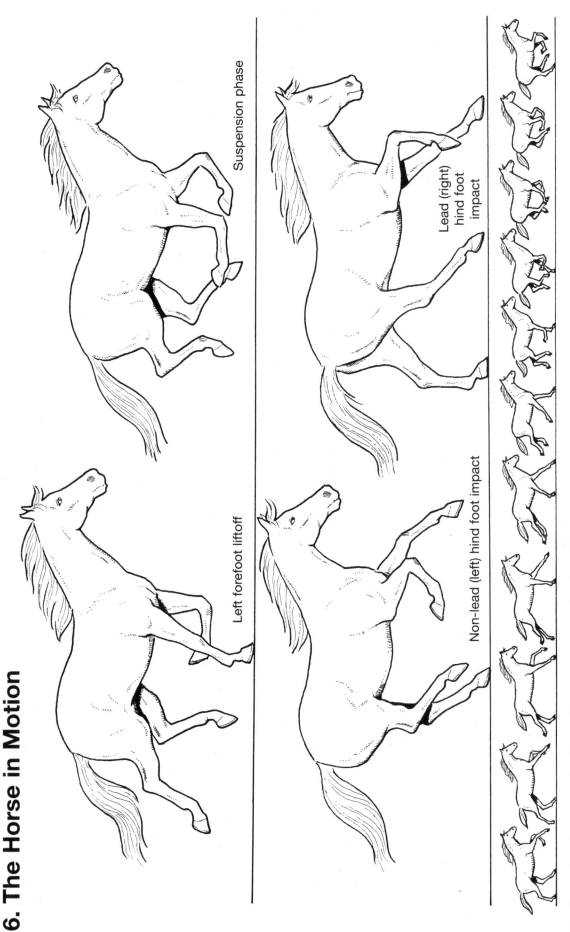

Suspension phase

Left forefoot liftoff

Lead (right) hind foot impact

Non-lead (left) hind foot impact

The horse has four natural gaits: walk, trot, canter, and gallop. The illustration shows the final and fastest gait—the gallop. The gallop consists of a rapid four-time step sequence, which varies according to the horse's speed. The left and right sides move in different manners, with one side leading, and the other side trailing. The four limbs move individually and in the following sequence of footfalls: non-lead hind foot, lead hind foot, non-lead forefoot, lead forefoot. One feature of the gallop is the suspension phase, when all four legs are off the ground. For years, people weren't sure if this actually happened, until a series of photographs taken in the nineteenth century by Edweard Muybridge proved conclusively that the horse was completely airborne for an instant during its stride. The suspension phase allows the horse to recover its equilibrium and to get its hind feet under the body. During the gallop there is one suspension phase per stride.

7. The Skeleton of the Horse

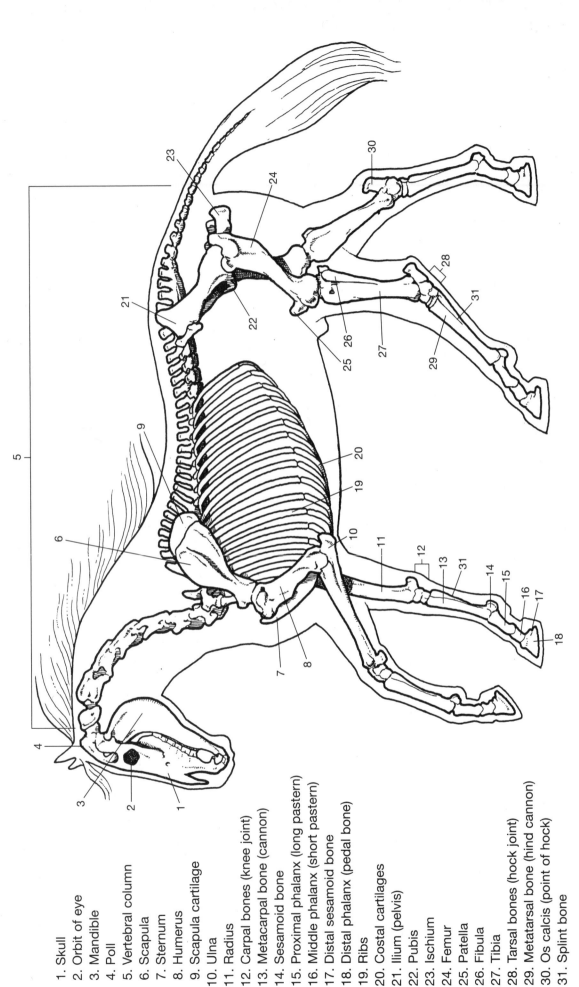

1. Skull
2. Orbit of eye
3. Mandible
4. Poll
5. Vertebral column
6. Scapula
7. Sternum
8. Humerus
9. Scapula cartilage
10. Ulna
11. Radius
12. Carpal bones (knee joint)
13. Metacarpal bone (cannon)
14. Sesamoid bone
15. Proximal phalanx (long pastern)
16. Middle phalanx (short pastern)
17. Distal sesamoid bone
18. Distal phalanx (pedal bone)
19. Ribs
20. Costal cartilages
21. Ilium (pelvis)
22. Pubis
23. Ischium
24. Femur
25. Patella
26. Fibula
27. Tibia
28. Tarsal bones (hock joint)
29. Metatarsal bone (hind cannon)
30. Os calcis (point of hock)
31. Splint bone

The skeleton is the framework of bones and other hard structures that support and protect the horse's soft tissues and vital organs. There are 205 bones in the normal adult horse skeleton, although some variation is possible, e.g. six or seven hock bones, and anywhere from fifteen to twenty-one tail vertebrae. There are twenty bones in each forelimb and twenty in each hind limb; they form the basis for locomotion and keeping them in good condition is of great importance in maintaining the health of the horse.

8. The Vertebral Column

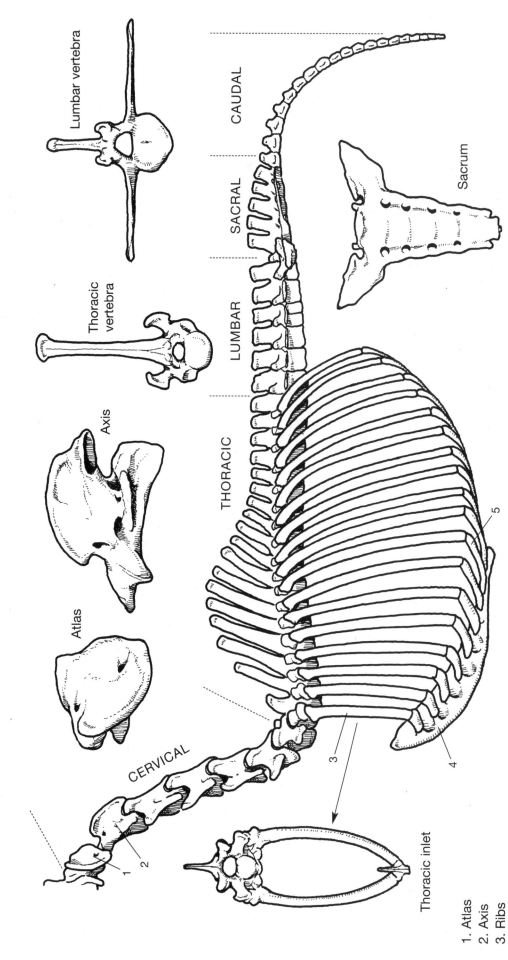

Lumbar vertebra

Thoracic vertebra

Axis

Atlas

CAUDAL

SACRAL

LUMBAR

THORACIC

Sacrum

CERVICAL

Thoracic inlet

3

2

1

4

5

1. Atlas
2. Axis
3. Ribs
4. Sternum
5. Costal cartilages

The horse has fifty-four bones in the vertebral column, arranged as follows: cervical, or neck vertebrae (7); thoracic, or chest vertebrae (18); lumbar, or loins vertebrae (6); sacrum, or croup bone (5) vertebrae fused to form a single bone); coccygeal, or tail vertebrae (18). However, the tail vertebrae can vary from fifteen to twenty-one. In addition, the horse has eighteen ribs on each side. Eight ribs are attached directly to the sternum by individual cartilaginous extensions. Ten false ribs are attached by cartilage to the posterior sternum. Cervical stenotic myelopathy (wobbler syndrome) causes spinal cord compression and is a common and devastating disease in horses. Most prevalent in thoroughbred and quarter horse males, it produces a loss of control in the hindquarters when the horse is walking or turning.

9. The Horse from the Front

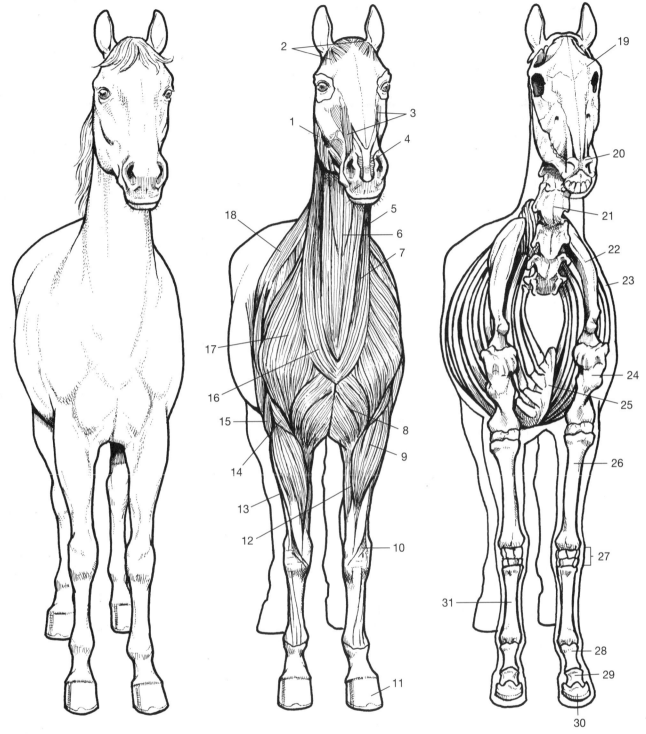

1. Masseter muscle
2. Rostral auricular muscles
3. Nasolabial levator muscles
4. Dorsal and ventral parts of the lateral nasal muscle
5. Jugular vein
6. Sternothyroid muscle
7. Sternomandibular muscle
8. Pectoral muscle
9. Radial carpal extensor muscles
10. Tendon of oblique carpal extensor
11. Hoof
12. Radial carpal flexor
13. Common digital extensor muscle
14. Brachial muscle
15. Deltoid muscle
16. Cutaneous superficial pectoral muscle
17. Brachiocephalic muscle
18. Trapezius muscle
19. Skull
20. Nasal cartilage
21. Cervical vertebrae
22. Scapula
23. Ribs
24. Humerus
25. Sternum
26. Radius
27. Carpal bones
28. Proximal phalanx (long pastern)
29. Middle phalanx (short pastern)
30. Distal phalanx (pedal bone)
31. Metacarpal bone (cannon)

10. The Horse from the Rear (Mare)

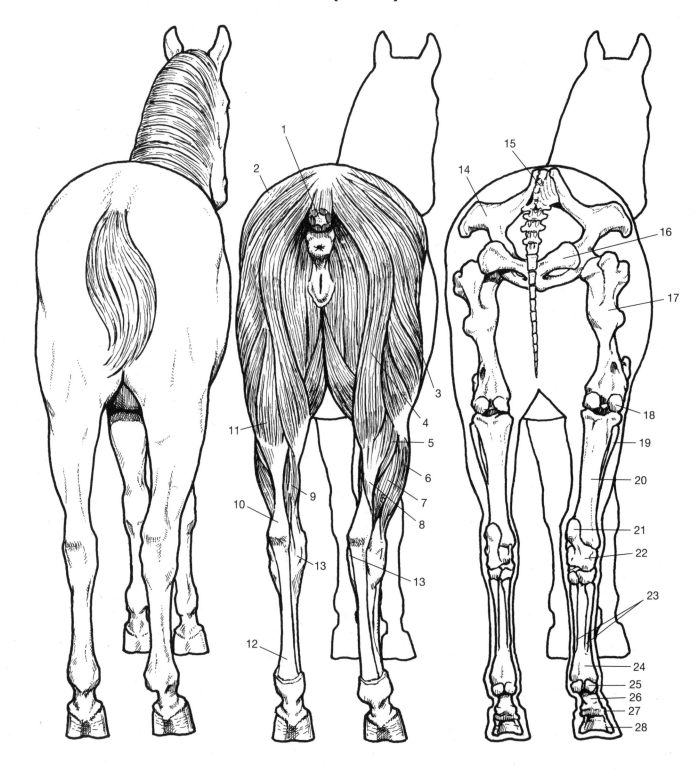

1. Tail muscles
2. Superficial gluteal muscle
3. Biceps femoris muscle
4. Semitendinous muscle
5. Soleus muscle
6. Lateral digital extensor muscle
7. Lateral head of deep digital flexor muscle
8. Tendon of gastrocnemius muscle
9. Superficial digital flexor muscle

10. Tendon of superficial digital flexor
11. Gastrocnemius muscle
12. Superficial and deep digital flexor tendons
13. Flexor retinaculum at hock
14. Wing of ilium
15. Sacral spinous process
16. Ischiatic arch
17. Femur
18. Lateral condyle of femur

19. Fibula
20. Tibia
21. Calcaneal tuber (point of hock)
22. Os calcis
23. Splint bones
24. Metatarsal (hind cannon)
25. Sesamoid bones
26. Proximal phalanx (long pastern)
27. Middle phalanx (short pastern)
28. Pedal bone

11. The Horse from Above

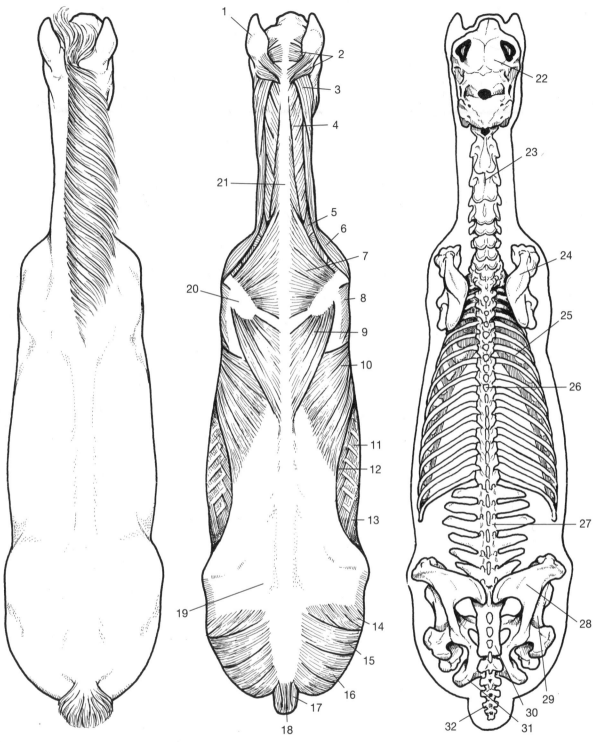

1. Auricular cartilage
2. Auricular muscles
3. Brachiocephalic muscle
4. Splenius muscle
5. Cervical part of ventral serrate muscle
6. Omotransverse muscle
7. Cervical trapezius muscle
8. Deltoid muscle
9. Thoracic trapezius muscle
10. Latissimus dorsi muscle

11. External intercostal muscles
12. Iliocostal muscles
13. External abdominal oblique muscle
14. Superficial gluteal muscle
15. Biceps femoris muscle
16. Semitendinous muscle
17. Short tail levator muscle
18. Long tail levator muscle
19. Thoracolumbar fascia
20. Scapular spine
21. Nuchal ligament

22. Skull
23. Cervical vertebrae
24. Scapula
25. Ribs
26. Thoracic vertebrae
27. Lumbar vertebrae
28. Ilium
29. Femur
30. Sacrum
31. Ischium
32. Caudal vertebrae

12. The Skull

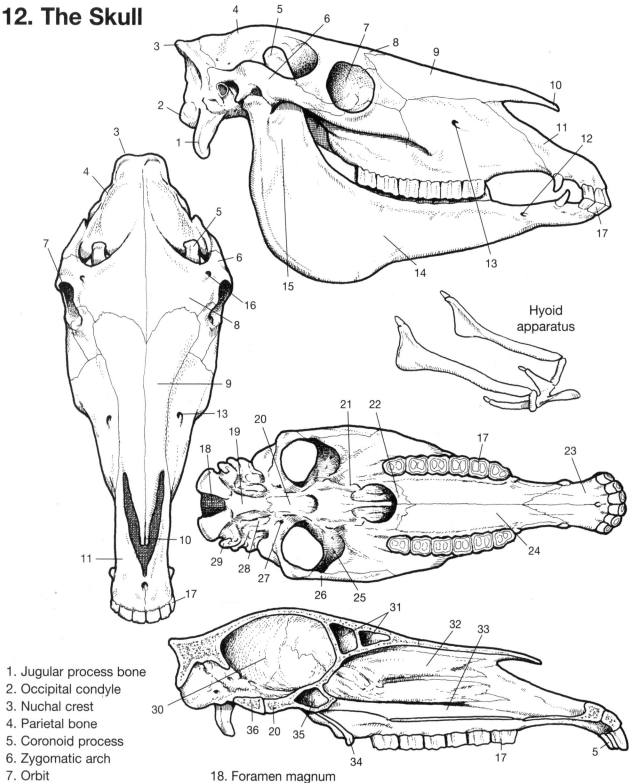

Hyoid apparatus

1. Jugular process bone
2. Occipital condyle
3. Nuchal crest
4. Parietal bone
5. Coronoid process
6. Zygomatic arch
7. Orbit
8. Frontal bone
9. Nasal bone
10. Nasal peak
11. Incisive bone
12. Mental foramen
13. Infraorbital foramen
14. Mandible
15. Ramus of the mandible
16. Supraorbital foramen
17. Teeth

18. Foramen magnum
19. Occipital bone
20. Basisphenoid bone
21. Hamulus of pterygoid bone
22. Palatine bone
23. Incisive bone
24. Maxilla
25. Orbital fissure
26. Zygomatic bone
27. Caudal alar foramen
28. Foramen lacerum

29. Jugular process bone
30. Cranial cavity
31. Conchofrontal sinus
32. Nasal cavity, middle nasal meatus
    and ventral nasal meatus, ventral
    nasal concha, and ethmoturbinates
33. Vomer
34. Pterygoid bone
35. Sphenopalatine sinus
36. Occipital bone

13. The Teeth

1. Maxilla, upper jaw
2. Sinuses
3. Reserve crown
4. Nasal bone
5. Wolf tooth
6. Crown
7. Apical foraminae
8. Apex
9. Mandible, lower jaw
10. Reserve crown
11. Table
12. Infundibulum
13. Dentine
14. Pulp cavity (dental star)
15. Peripheral Cement

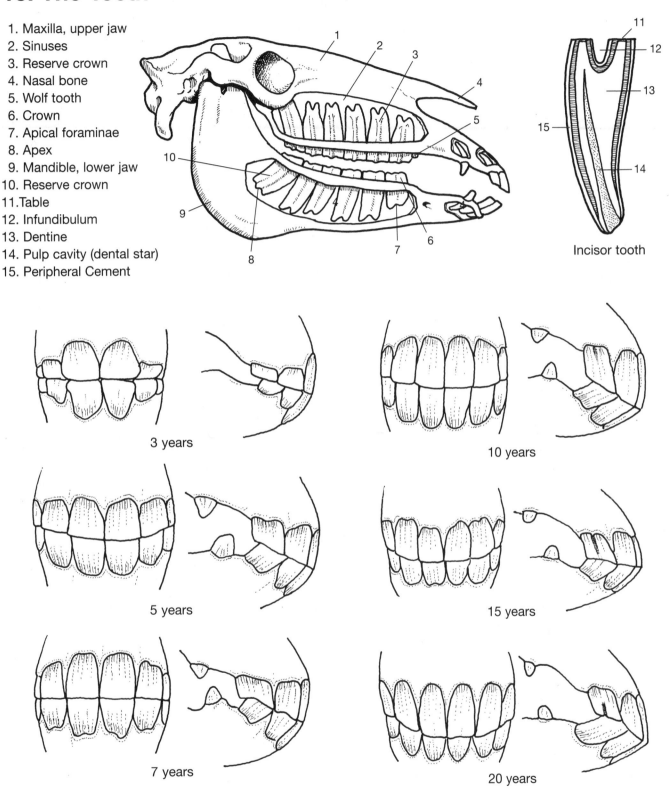

Incisor tooth

3 years

5 years

7 years

10 years

15 years

20 years

An adult horse has a total of forty teeth, which have long roots. The molar "sets" are very close to one another, with no gaps. This tight structure helps the teeth withstand the considerable forces placed upon them. As a result of continual friction in the upper and lower jaws during grinding of food, the surface or "table," is worn down by approximately 3mm (1/5 inch) each year. The articulation between the equine jaws permits considerable lateral movement, as well as forward and backward movement of the lower jaw, enabling the molars to grind food thoroughly. The appearance of the incisor teeth, their profiles and tables can be used to estimate the age of a horse. This can be done with some accuracy up to the age of seven; beyond this only an approximate estimate is possible. Horses over the age of six are often described as "aged."

14. Superficial Structures of the Head

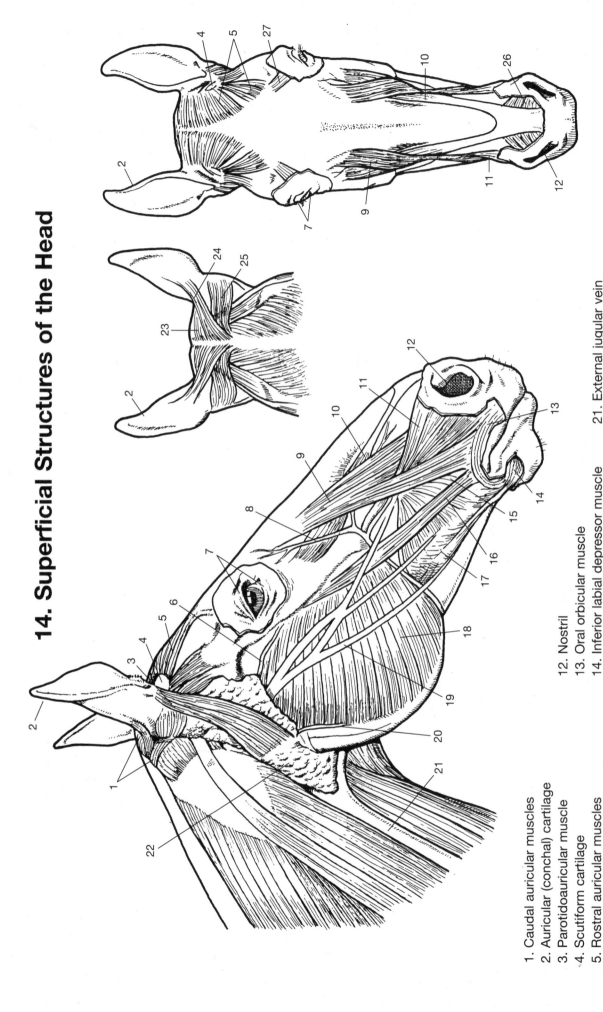

1. Caudal auricular muscles
2. Auricular (conchal) cartilage
3. Parotidoauricular muscle
4. Scutiform cartilage
5. Rostral auricular muscles
6. Transverse facial artery, vein and nerve
7. Eyelids
8. Angular artery and vein of the eye
9. Nasolabial levator muscle
10. Superior labial levator muscle
11. Canine muscle
12. Nostril
13. Oral orbicular muscle
14. Inferior labial depressor muscle
15. Buccinator muscle
16. Zygomatic muscle
17. Facial cutaneous muscle
18. Masseter muscle
19. Facial nerve
20. Masseteric artery and vein
21. External jugular vein
22. Parotid salivary gland
23. Interscutular muscle
24. Levator muscle
25. Abductor muscle
26. Dorsal and ventral parts of lateral nasal muscle
27. Levator muscle of medial angle of eye.

15. The Internal Structures and Cavities of the Head

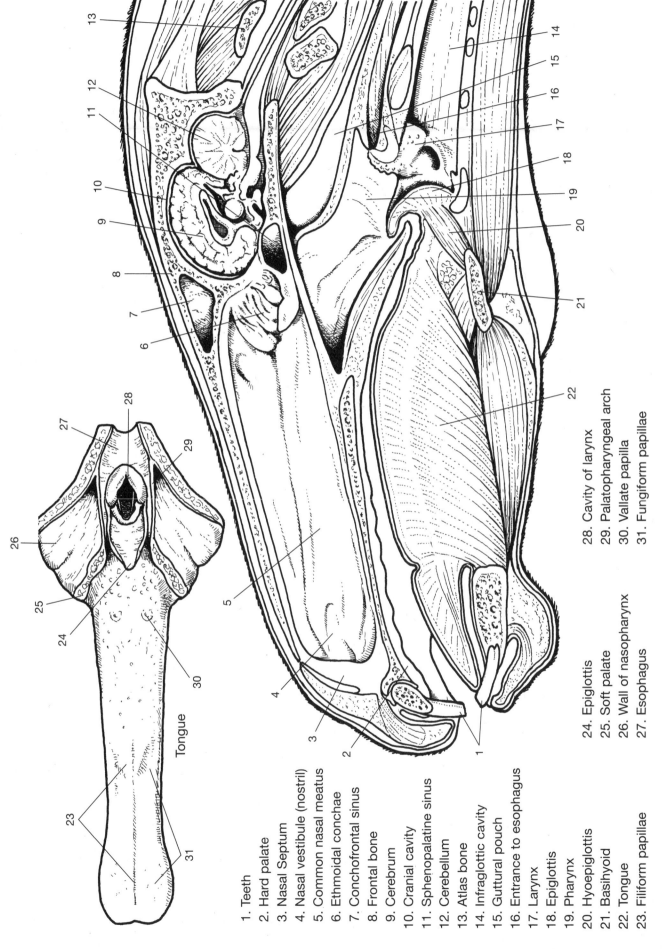

1. Teeth
2. Hard palate
3. Nasal Septum
4. Nasal vestibule (nostril)
5. Common nasal meatus
6. Ethmoidal conchae
7. Conchofrontal sinus
8. Frontal bone
9. Cerebrum
10. Cranial cavity
11. Sphenopalatine sinus
12. Cerebellum
13. Atlas bone
14. Infraglottic cavity
15. Guttural pouch
16. Entrance to esophagus
17. Larynx
18. Epiglottis
19. Pharynx
20. Hyoepiglottis
21. Basihyoid
22. Tongue
23. Filiform papillae
24. Epiglottis
25. Soft palate
26. Wall of nasopharynx
27. Esophagus
28. Cavity of larynx
29. Palatopharyngeal arch
30. Vallate papilla
31. Fungiform papillae

Tongue

16. The Eye

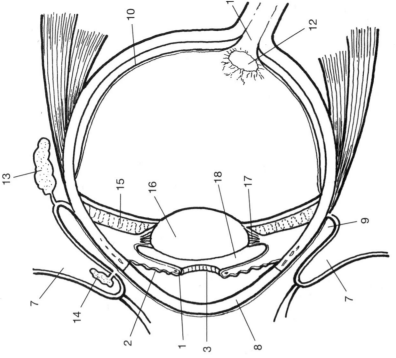

1. Corpora nigra
2. Iris
3. Pupil
4. White of eye
5. Third eyelid
6. Lacrimal caruncle
7. Eyelids
8. Cornea
9. Conjunctiva

10. Retina
11. Optic nerve
12. Optic disc
13. Lacrimal gland
14. Tarsal gland
15. Ciliary ring
16. Lens
17. Ciliary muscle
18. Posterior chamber

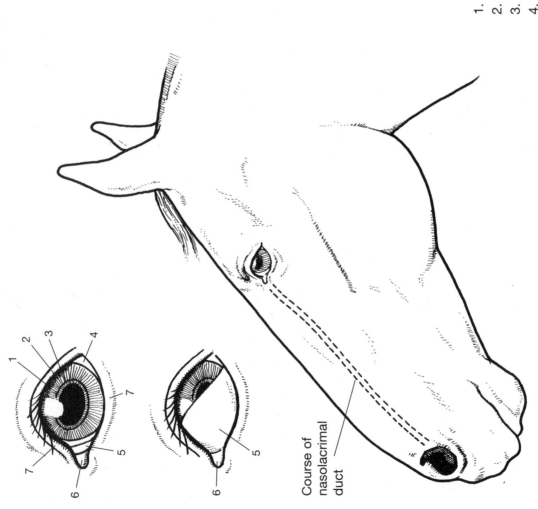

Course of nasolacrimal duct

The eye should be clear, with salmon-pink mucous membranes indicating a healthy blood supply. Tears secreted by the lacrimal gland and the gland of the third eyelid wash over the surface of the eye, collecting at the junction of the lids. Tears then flow through the two lacrimal puncta and lacrimal canals into the lacrimal sac and continue into the nasolacrimal duct.

17. The Foot

Proper condition of the legs and feet are crucial to the health and soundness of a horse, for major problems can develop in these parts of the horse's anatomy. It is essential to regularly check the condition of the horse's feet.

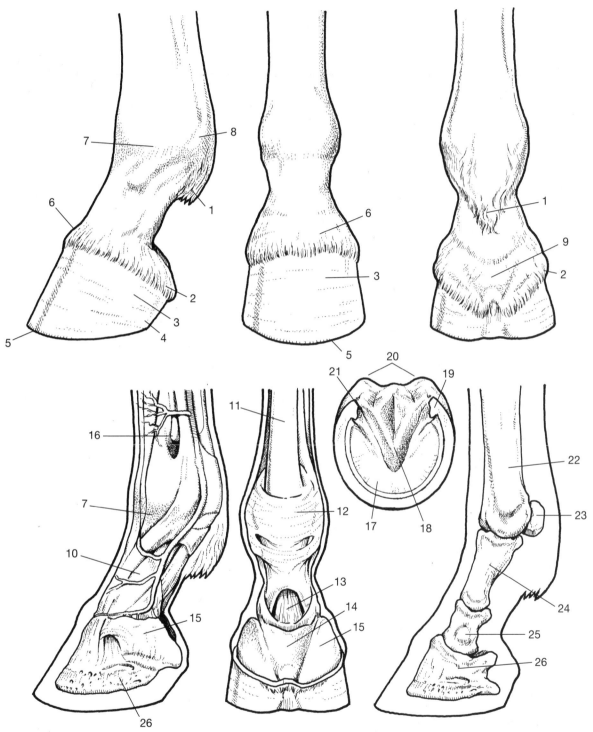

1. Fetlock tuft
2. Peripole
3. Wall
4. Heel
5. Toe
6. Coronet
7. Fetlock joint
8. Site of lateral digital vein and artery
9. Interbulbar furrow
10. Sesamoid bone
11. Flexor tendon
12. Ligament of fetlock
13. Deep flexor tendon
14. Plantar cushion
15. Lateral cartilage
16. Metacarpal bone
17. Sole
18. Frog
19. Angle of wall
20. Bulb of heels
21. Collateral groove
22. Metacarpal bone (cannon)
23. Sesamoid bone
24. Proximal phalanx (large pastern)
25. Middle phalanx (small pastern)
26. Distal phalanx (pedal bone)

18. The Forelimb

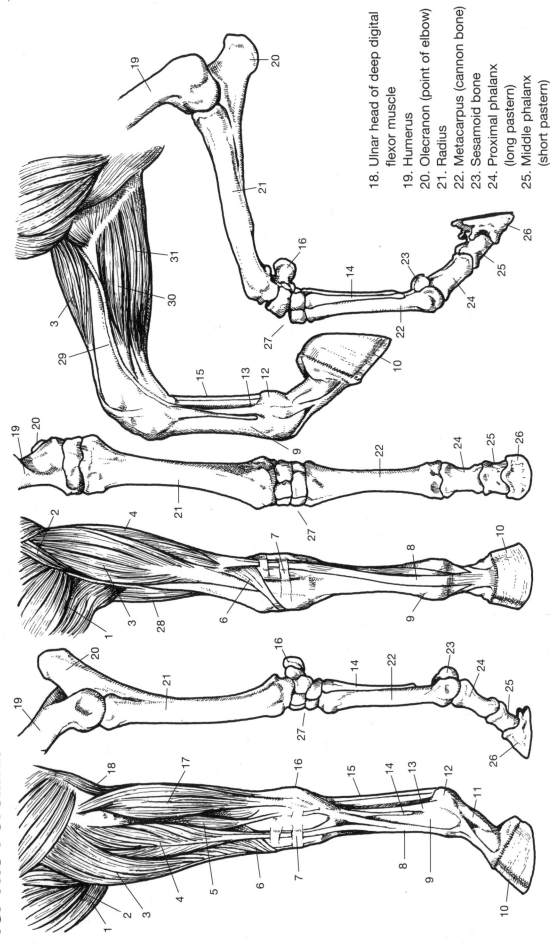

18. Ulnar head of deep digital
    flexor muscle
19. Humerus
20. Olecranon (point of elbow)
21. Radius
22. Metacarpus (cannon bone)
23. Sesamoid bone
24. Proximal phalanx
    (long pastern)
25. Middle phalanx
    (short pastern)
26. Pedal bone
27. Carpal bones (knee joint)
28. Radial carpal flexor muscle
29. Great subcutaneous vein
30. Radial carpal flexor muscle
31. Ulnar carpal flexor muscle

13. Suspensory ligament
14. Splint bone
15. Superficial and deep digital
    flexor tendons
16. Accessory carpal bone (pisiform)
17. Lateral ulnar muscle

7. Extensor retinaculum
8. Digital extensor tendon
9. Metacarpal bone, cannon
10. Hoof
11. Proximal digital annular ligament
12. Palmar annular ligament of the fetlock

1. Descending pectoral muscle
2. Brachial muscle
3. Radial carpal extensor muscle
4. Common digital extensor muscle
5. Lateral digital extensor muscle
6. Oblique carpal extensor muscle

19. The Hind Limb

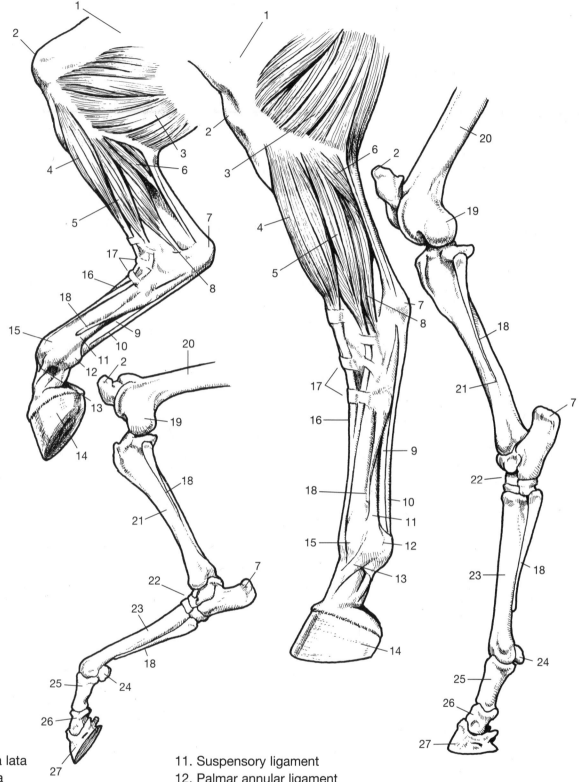

1. Fascia lata
2. Patella
3. Femoris biceps muscles
4. Long digital extensor muscle
5. Lateral digital extensor muscle
6. Gastrocnemius muscle
7. Point of hock
8. Deep digital flexor muscle
9. Deep digital flexor tendon
10. Superficial digital flexor tendon

11. Suspensory ligament
12. Palmar annular ligament
13. Extensor branch of suspensory
    ligament
14. Hoof
15. Fetlock
16. Tendon of long digital extensor
17. Annular ligaments
18. Split bone
19. Lateral condyle of tibia

20. Femur
21. Tibia
22. Tarsal bones
23. Metatarsal (hind cannon)
24. Sesamoid bone
25. Proximal phalanx (long pastern)
26. Middle phalanx (short pastern)
27. Distal phalanx (pedal bone)

20. The Internal Organs of the Horse

Most of the horse's internal organs work in the same way as those of other mammals. The liver is the animal's largest organ, weighing an average of 11lbs. Its secretion of bile is delivered directly to the duodenum by the bile duct, since the horse lacks a gall bladder for storing bile. The stomach of the horse is very small for the animal's size. The illustration shows the left side of a mare and the right side of a stallion.

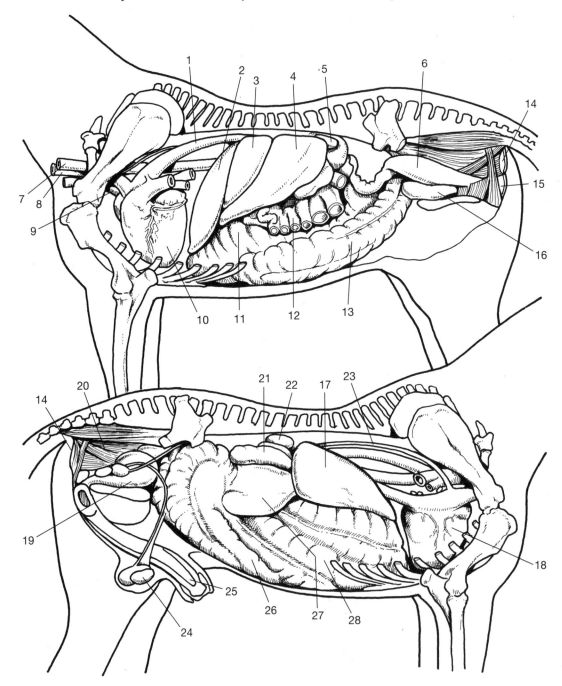

1. Aorta	11. Left dorsal colon	21. Descending duodenum
2. Left lobe of the liver	12. Small intestine	22. Right kidney
3. Stomach	13. Left ventral colon	23. Azygos vein
4. Spleen	14. External anal sphincter	24. Right testicle
5. Left kidney	15. Vulva	25. Body of penis
6. Body of the uterus	16. Urinary bladder	26. Lateral caecal band
7. Esophagus	17. Right lobe of liver	27. Dorsal sac of caecum
8. Trachea	18. Right ventricle of heart	28. Right ventral colon
9. Left vagus nerve	19. Urinary bladder	
10. Left ventricle of the heart	20. Rectum	

21. The Cardiovascular System

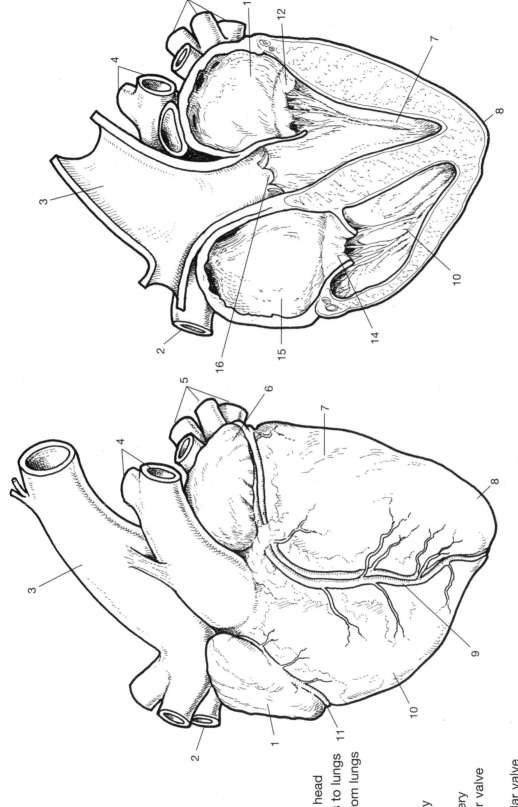

1. Right auricle
2. Cranial vena cava
3. Aorta to body and head
4. Pulmonary arteries to lungs
5. Pulmonary veins from lungs
6. Left auricle
7. Left ventricle
8. Apex
9. Left coronary artery
10. Right ventricle
11. Right coronary artery
12. Left atrioventricular valve
13. Left atrium
14. Right atrioventricular valve
15. Right atrium
16. Cusp of aortic valve

The horse's heart consists of four chambers with four sets of valves. The heart pumps blood into the arteries, which extend to all parts of the body. The blood returns to the heart via the veins. The resting heart rate of a healthy adult horse varies from horse to horse, and from breed to breed. On the average, a horse's heart rate is between thirty-six and forty-two beats per minute.

22. The Cardiovascular System (continued)

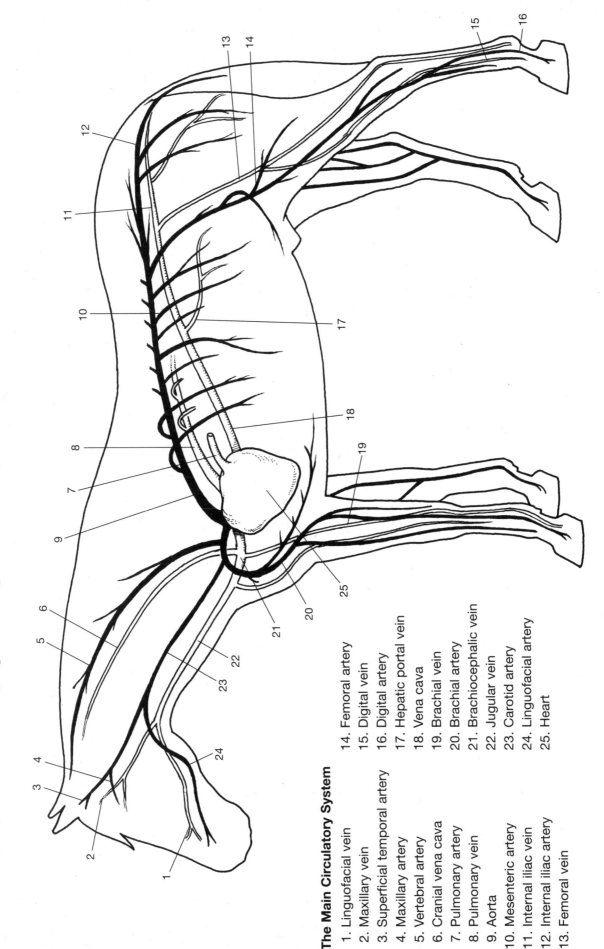

The Main Circulatory System

1. Linguofacial vein
2. Maxillary vein
3. Superficial temporal artery
4. Maxillary artery
5. Vertebral artery
6. Cranial vena cava
7. Pulmonary artery
8. Pulmonary vein
9. Aorta
10. Mesenteric artery
11. Internal iliac vein
12. Internal iliac artery
13. Femoral vein
14. Femoral artery
15. Digital vein
16. Digital artery
17. Hepatic portal vein
18. Vena cava
19. Brachial vein
20. Brachial artery
21. Brachiocephalic vein
22. Jugular vein
23. Carotid artery
24. Linguofacial artery
25. Heart

23. The Nervous System

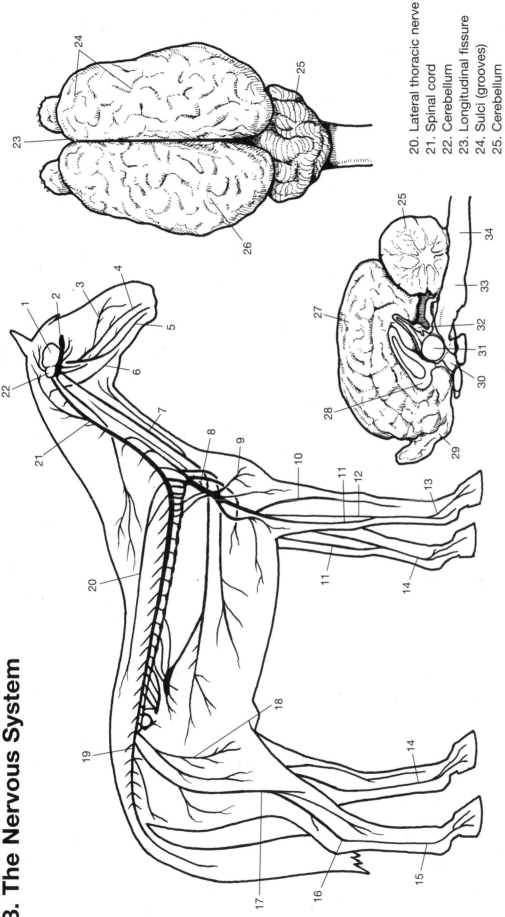

The Principal Nerves and the Nervous System

The nervous system is the communications network of the horse's body. It consists of two parts: the central nervous system, made up of brain and spinal cord, and the peripheral nervous system, consisting of nerves radiating from the spinal cord to muscles, internal organs, and skin. Sensations from outside the body, as well as impulses from internal organs and other tissues, are sent to the brain and interpreted. The brain then reacts appropriately.

1. Cerebrum
2. Olfactory bulb
3. Facial nerve
4. Branch of trigeminal nerve
5. Branch of trigeminal nerve
6. Hyperglossal nerve
7. Vagus nerve
8. Brachial plexus
9. Pectoral nerve

10. Radial nerve
11. Ulnar nerve
12. Median nerve
13. Lateral palmar nerve
14. Medial plantar nerve
15. Lateral plantar nerve
16. Tibial nerve
17. Sciatic nerve
18. Femoral nerve
19. Lumbosacral nerve

20. Lateral thoracic nerve
21. Spinal cord
22. Cerebellum
23. Longitudinal fissure
24. Sulci (grooves)
25. Cerebellum
26. Gyri (convolutions)
27. Right cerebral hemisphere
28. Corpus callosum
29. Olfactory bulb
30. Hypothalamus
31. Thalamus
32. Pineal gland
33. Pons
34. Medulla oblongata

24. The Respiratory System

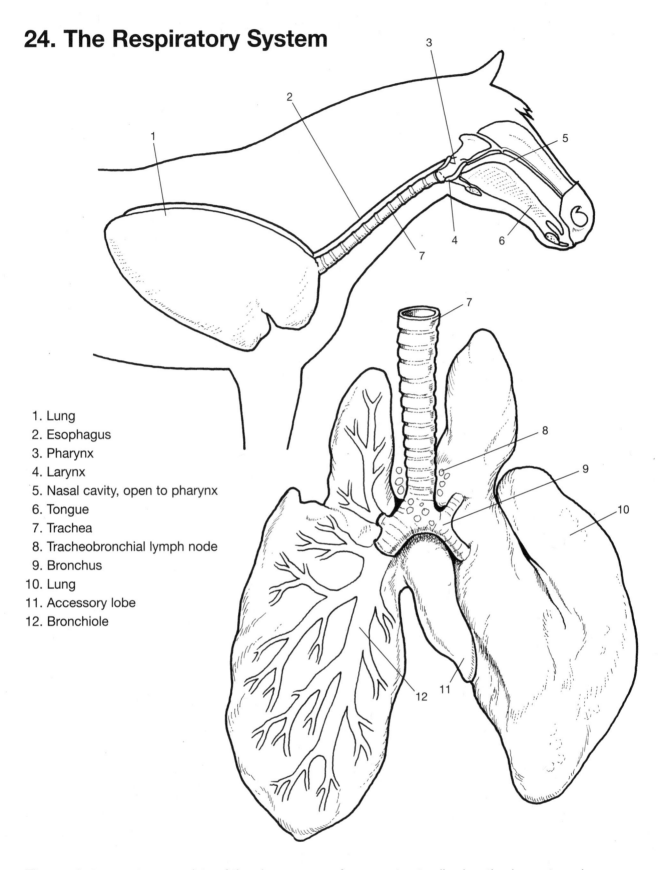

1. Lung
2. Esophagus
3. Pharynx
4. Larynx
5. Nasal cavity, open to pharynx
6. Tongue
7. Trachea
8. Tracheobronchial lymph node
9. Bronchus
10. Lung
11. Accessory lobe
12. Bronchiole

The respiratory system consists of the air passages of the head, nostrils to pharynx, the pharynx, trachea or windpipe, bronchi, and lungs. The lungs are the two organs in which oxygen and carbon dioxide are exchanged between the blood and the air. The lungs are situated in the chest cavity known as the thorax, the walls (ribs and diaphragm) of which can expand or contract, allowing the lungs to enlarge or compress. Movements of the chest alternately draw in and expel air from the lungs. The normal breathing rate of a standing horse at rest is eight to sixteen breaths a minute. The rate may be affected by excitement, exercise, age, size, environmental temperature, pregnancy, and/or a full digestive tract.

25. The Horse's Pulse, Signs of Health

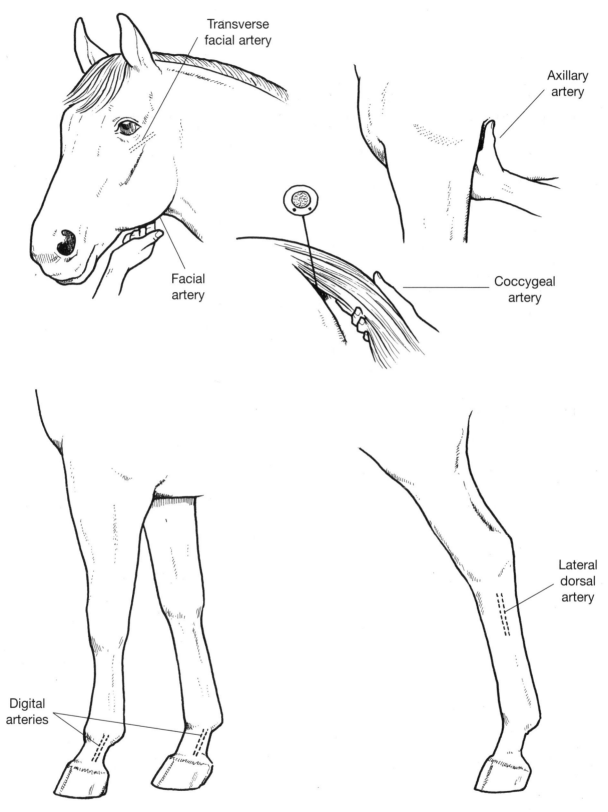

Transverse facial artery

Axillary artery

Facial artery

Coccygeal artery

Lateral dorsal artery

Digital arteries

To recognize when a horse is unwell, it is important to know the signs of a healthy horse, both physical and behavioral. These signs are: appearance, behavior, and condition. A healthy horse is bright-eyed, has a shine to its coat, stands equally on all four feet, and is alert, with ears warm to the touch at their bases. Heart rate and temperature should be checked regularly. A horse's normal breathing rate varies from about eight to sixteen breaths a minute. The heart rate is typically 36—42 beats a minute. Temperature is usually 37.8–38.3 degrees centigrade (100–101 degrees Fahrenheit). The pulse may be felt through the skin over certain arteries; the pulse may be taken at these sites.

26. The Digestive System

1. Anus
2. Rectum
3. Base of caecum
4. Small intestine (20 meters long)
5. Kidney
6. Buccal cavity
7. Esophagus
8. Liver
9. Large colon (3.4 meters long)
10. Caecum
11. Small colon

12. Aorta
13. Caudal vena cava
14. Right kidney
15. Duodenum
16. Stomach
17. Pancreas
18. Adrenal gland
19. Left kidney
20. Esophagus
21. Portal vein
22. Hepatic artery
23. Hepatic duct

Most of the horse's internal organs work in the same way as those of other mammals, but the horse has three unique features in the digestive system which distinguish it from other mammals. These are (1) the greatest volume of the alimentary tract is at the rear, where the major digestive processes take place; (2) the stomach is very small for the animal's size; and (3) there is no gall bladder. The reason for this is because the horse needs a constant supply of bile, as it is a continuous feeder.

27. The Urinary System

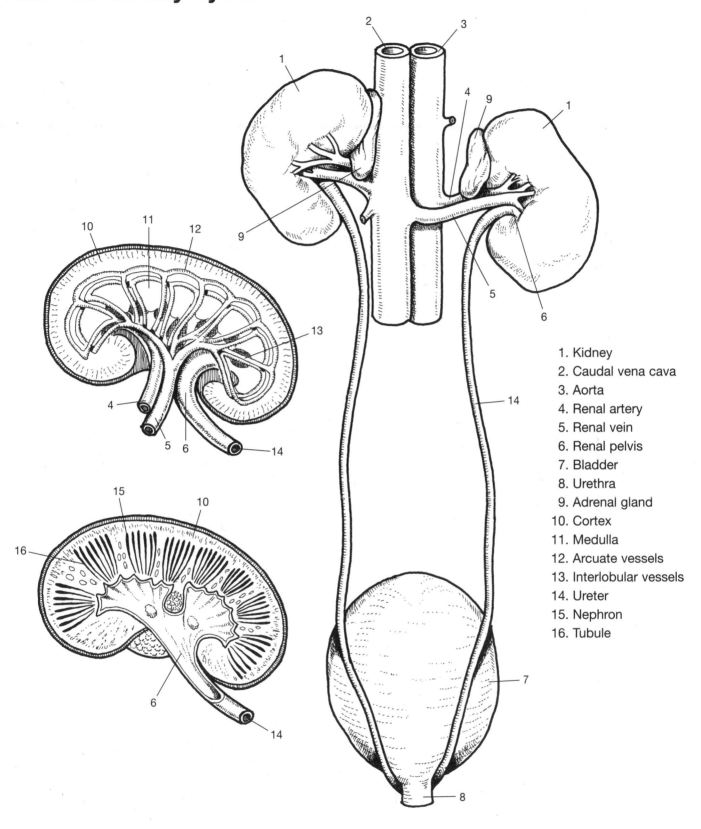

1. Kidney
2. Caudal vena cava
3. Aorta
4. Renal artery
5. Renal vein
6. Renal pelvis
7. Bladder
8. Urethra
9. Adrenal gland
10. Cortex
11. Medulla
12. Arcuate vessels
13. Interlobular vessels
14. Ureter
15. Nephron
16. Tubule

The horse, like all mammals, has two kidneys, whose function is to filter the blood and form urine. The urine passes to the bladder through the ureters and from there the urine passes to the outside through the urethra. The urethra has a common exit from the body with the sexual tract, the vagina in the mare, and the penis in the stallion. A horse produces up to ten liters (2½ gallons) of urine daily, the color and consistency of which vary in everyday situations. Normal equine urine is cloudy and yellow in color. Urine samples are important laboratory aids to clinical diagnosis.

28. The Reproductive System

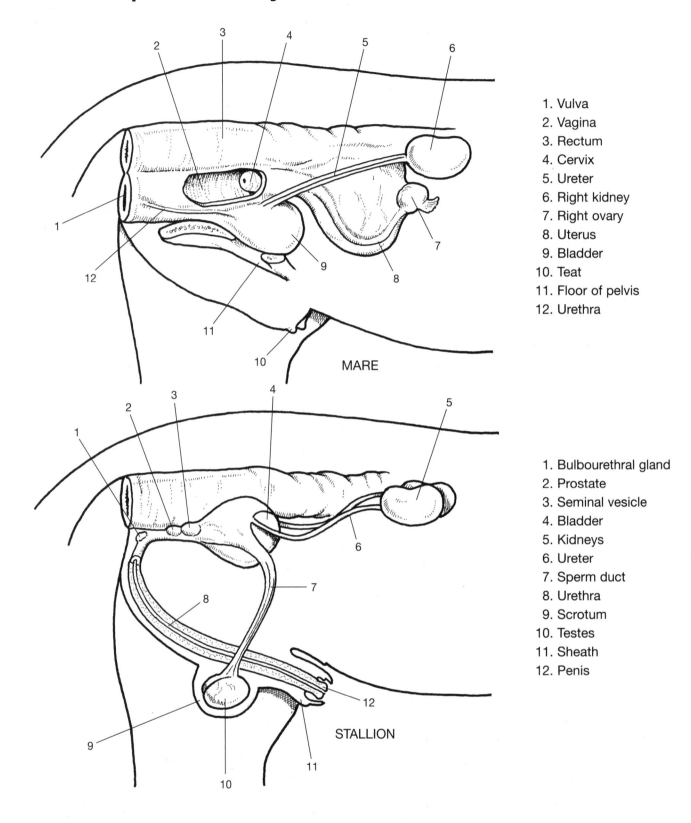

MARE

1. Vulva
2. Vagina
3. Rectum
4. Cervix
5. Ureter
6. Right kidney
7. Right ovary
8. Uterus
9. Bladder
10. Teat
11. Floor of pelvis
12. Urethra

STALLION

1. Bulbourethral gland
2. Prostate
3. Seminal vesicle
4. Bladder
5. Kidneys
6. Ureter
7. Sperm duct
8. Urethra
9. Scrotum
10. Testes
11. Sheath
12. Penis

The genital organs of the mare consist of two ovaries and oviducts or fallopian tubes, the uterus, cervix, vagina, and vulva. The ovaries are responsible for producing the female sex cell, i.e. the egg, or ovum. The stallion's sex organs consist of two testes (housed in the scrotum) in which spermatozoa are produced; collecting ducts which connect with the urethra after traveling in the spermatic cord with arteries and veins; the accessory glands comprising the prostate, seminal vesicles, bulbourethral gland, and penis. The penis is housed in the prepuce or "sheath."

29. Foaling

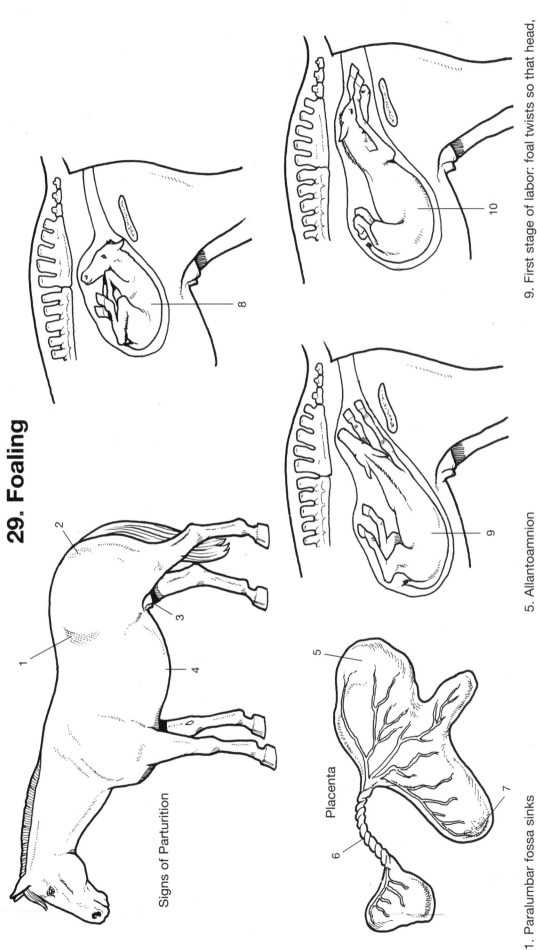

Signs of Parturition

Placenta

1. Paralumbar fossa sinks
2. Softening and relaxation of muscles and ligaments around tailhead
3. Waxing of teats
4. Enlarged abdomen

5. Allantoamnion
6. Umbilical cord
7. Cervical star
8. Position of foal during late pregnancy

9. First stage of labor: foal twists so that head, neck, and chest are in the proper position
10. As the second stage of labor progresses, forelegs and head enter the pelvic girdle, followed by the chest

The length of gestation (duration of pregnancy) in the mare is eleven months. There are several signs of impending parturition (the process of giving birth): enlarged and dropped abdomen, sinking in at the paralumbar fossa, relaxation and softening of the muscles and ligaments adjacent to the tailhead, filling of the udder with colostrum, and "waxing" of teats due to excessive secretion by oil glands at openings. These signs usually occur around forty-eight hours before parturition.

30. Conformation

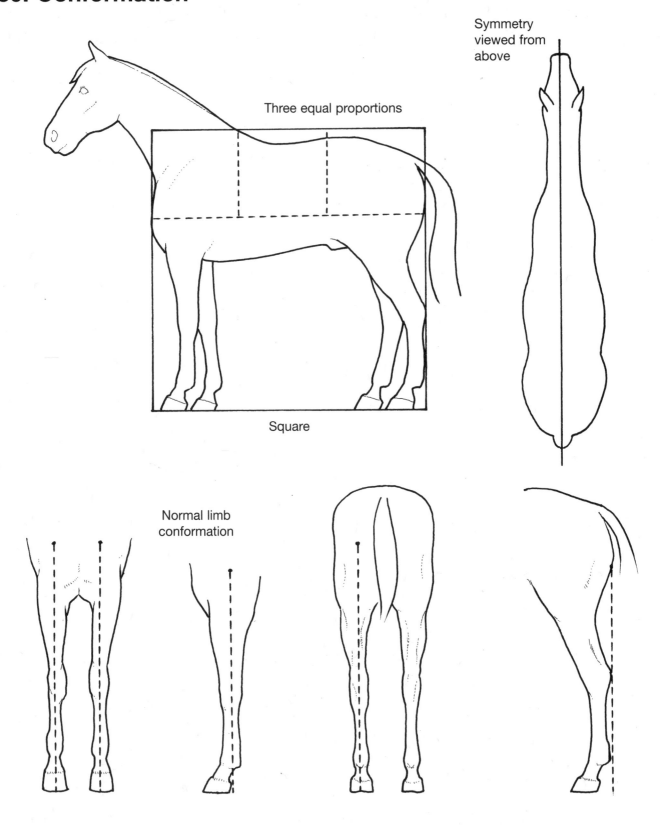

Three equal proportions

Square

Symmetry viewed from above

Normal limb conformation

A horse's conformation is its overall makeup and shape, as determined by its skeletal outline. What constitutes ideal conformation varies according to the work the horse is required to do. Allowing for these variations, basic guidelines can be used when looking for desirable conformation. These relate to proportion: if a horse is correctly proportioned, it will be better balanced and more able to perform its allotted tasks than a horse with less harmonious proportions. A poor or average conformation warns of the likelihood of sub-optimal performance, risk of injury, and reduced durability.